THE HISTORY OF CORVETTES

SETH HINGSTON

PowerKiDS press.

NEW YORK

Published in 2019 by The Rosen Publishing Group, Inc.
29 East 21st Street, New York, NY 10010

First Edition

Editor: Elizabeth Krajnik
Book Design: Michael Flynn

Photo Credits: Cover (car) Ed Aldridge/Shutterstock.com; cover, p. 1 (emblem) Atomazul/Shutterstock.com; cover, pp. 1, 3–8, 10–14, 16, 18–24, 26–32 (background) fotomak/Shutterstock.com; p. 5 (car) PaulLP/Shutterstock.com; p. 5 (museum) Roman Korotkov/Shutterstock.com; p. 6 Bettmann/Getty Images; p. 7 Raymond Boyd/Michael Ochs Archives/Getty Images; p. 8 VanderWolf Images/Shutterstock.com; p. 9 Steve Lagreca/Shutterstock.com; p. 11 (main) Kevork Djansezian/Getty Images News/Getty Images; p. 11 (inset) Zoran Karapancev/Shutterstock.com; p. 13 Brian Cleary/Getty Images Sport/Getty Images; p. 15 Robert Laberge/Getty Images Sport/Getty Images; p. 16 Dean Mouhtaropoulos/Getty Images Sport/Getty Images; p. 17 Antoine Antoniol/Getty Images News/Getty Images; p. 18 Grzegorz Czapski/Shutterstock.com; p. 19 Heritage Images/Hulton Archive/Getty Images; p. 21 (main) Yevgen Belich/Shutterstock.com; p. 21 (inset) The Enthusiast Network/Getty Images; p. 23 Art Konovalov/Shutterstock.com; p. 25 (main) Rob Wilson/Shutterstock.com; p. 25 (inset) Darrell Ingham/Getty Images Sport/Getty Images; p. 27 (main) Darren Brode/Shutterstock.com; p. 27 (inset) Roberto Lusso/Shutterstock.com; pp. 28–29 Boykov/Shutterstock.com.

Library of Congress Cataloging-in-Publication Data

Names: Kingston, Seth, author.
Title: The history of Corvettes / Seth Kingston.
Description: New York : PowerKids Press, [2019] | Series: Under the hood | Includes index.
Identifiers: LCCN 2018027011| ISBN 9781538343371 (library bound) | ISBN 9781538344507 (pbk.) | ISBN 9781538344514 (6 pack)
Subjects: LCSH: Corvette automobile–History–Juvenile literature.
Classification: LCC TL215.C6 K544 2019 | DDC 629.222/2–dc23
LC record available at https://lccn.loc.gov/2018027011

Manufactured in the United States of America

CPSIA Compliance Information: Batch #CWPK19: For Further Information contact Rosen Publishing, New York, New York at 1-800-237-9932

CONTENTS

AN AMERICAN CLASSIC

American car manufacturer Chevrolet is the creator of one of the country's most iconic cars—the Corvette. Since Chevrolet produced the first Corvette in 1953, the Corvette has established itself as a leader in the sports car market. Chevrolet has sold more than 1.5 million Corvettes as of 2009.

The Corvette's **design** was inspired by European sports cars, and it was made to compete with and beat European sports cars on the racetrack. Corvettes are built to be high-performance cars. However, unlike many European sports cars, such as Ferraris and Lamborghinis, they're produced in ways that keep them affordable. Its cool design and great performance combined with its affordability give the Corvette a wide appeal.

Today, Corvette enthusiasts can explore the history of this American classic at the National Corvette Museum in Bowling Green, Kentucky.

THE CORVETTE IS THE LONGEST-RUNNING, CONTINUOUSLY PRODUCED **PASSENGER** CAR IN THE WORLD.

NATIONAL
CORVETTE MUSEUM
ENTRANCE

COMPETING WITH FORD

In 1911, Louis Chevrolet and William C. Durant founded Chevrolet in Detroit, Michigan. They wanted their company to compete with Ford and its new car, the Model T. In 1915, Chevrolet introduced its first model that could truly compete with the Model T. It was called the Chevrolet Model 490. It cost $490, which was $5 less than the Model T cost. In 1918, Chevrolet joined General Motors.

LOUIS CHEVROLET

START YOUR ENGINES

IN 2006, THE THIRD 1953 CORVETTE PRODUCED WAS SOLD FOR $1.06 MILLION. FOR THAT MUCH MONEY, YOU COULD BUY 13 CORVETTE Z06s FROM 2018!

Chevrolet produced the first Corvette in 1953 in Flint, Michigan. Harley Earl was one of the people behind the Corvette's design. Earl knew that to compete with European sports cars, the Corvette had to be eye-catching and stylish. All 1953 models were Polo White convertibles with Sportsman Red interiors, or inner parts. Each cost $3,498. Chevrolet only made 300 of these Corvettes.

FOR THE FIRST 10 YEARS CHEVROLET PRODUCED THE CORVETTE, IT ONLY CAME AS A CONVERTIBLE.

FROM SIX TO EIGHT CYLINDERS

The first Corvettes came with an inline six-**cylinder** engine. Then, in 1955, a V-8 engine became a choice, and the majority of buyers bought Corvettes with those. A V-8 engine is an engine that has eight cylinders arranged in a "V" shape. In 1956, Chevrolet stopped producing Corvettes with the inline six-cylinder engines. The more cylinders an engine has, the more powerful it is. Non-sports cars often have only four or six cylinders. Having eight cylinders makes the engine roar as the driver accelerates, or goes faster.

V-8 ENGINE

TODAY, BUYERS CAN CHANGE A LOT OF THINGS ABOUT THEIR CORVETTE. THEY CAN CHOOSE DIFFERENT PAINT COLORS, **TRANSMISSION** TYPES, OR WHETHER THEY WANT A CONVERTIBLE OR A COUPE, OR HARDTOP.

The Corvette is known for its innovation. That means that, over the years, Chevrolet has introduced many new things, such as the latest **technology** and design, for the cars. These changes have kept Corvettes among the fastest, most powerful, and most stylish cars on the road.

MANY TO CHOOSE FROM

Today, buyers can choose from a number of Corvette models to fit their needs and wants. In 2019, there were four models of Corvettes produced. They are the Stingray, the Grand Sport, the Z06, and the ZR1. Even though most Corvettes cost less than half of what European sports cars such as Ferraris cost, they're just as powerful under the hood. The 2019 Z06 has 650 horsepower and the 2019 ZR1 has 755 horsepower!

The 2019 Corvette Stingray can go from 0 to 60 miles (0 to 96.6 km) per hour in just 3.7 seconds. Starting at $121,000, the 2019 ZR1 can go from 0 to 60 miles (0 to 96.6 km) per hour in just 2.85 seconds and can reach a top speed of 212 miles (341.2 km) per hour!

AS OF 2019, THE CORVETTE IS IN ITS SEVENTH GENERATION OF PRODUCTION. THE SEVENTH GENERATION (C7) MODELS WERE RELEASED BEGINNING IN 2014.

2019 ZR1

TWENTY SEASONS OF RACING

In 2018, the Corvette Racing program entered its 20th season. While production Corvettes are built for personal enjoyment, special Corvettes are made for their power out on the track. In 1999, the Corvette C5-R made its debut, or first appearance, at the 24 Hours of Daytona. Throughout the next five years, Corvette Racing collected 31 victories in the American Le Mans Series, or ALMS. These victories helped drivers such as Ron Fellows become famous in the racing world.

Since 2014, Corvette Racing drivers have raced the C7.R. This model is based on the 2015 Chevrolet Corvette Z06. The frames for the Z06 and the C7.R are made at the same plant in Bowling Green, Kentucky. C7.Rs make fewer pit stops during long-distance races than previous models.

THERE ARE MANY SIMILARITIES BETWEEN THE CORVETTES YOU CAN BUY FROM A CHEVROLET DEALERSHIP AND THOSE YOU CAN FIND ON RACETRACKS.

START YOUR ENGINES

IN 2016, CORVETTE RACING CELEBRATED THE 60TH ANNIVERSARY OF THE CORVETTE'S FIRST **PROFESSIONAL** RACE. IN 1956, FIVE CORVETTES COMPETED AT THE 12 HOURS OF SEBRING HELD AT SEBRING INTERNATIONAL RACEWAY IN FLORIDA.

PACE CARS

A pace car is a car that doesn't actually race but leads all the racecars around the track for a warm-up lap and pulls off the track before they start racing. Corvettes have served as pace cars for the Indianapolis 500 more than any other car in history. As of the 102nd running of the Indianapolis 500 in 2018, Corvettes have served as pace cars for the race 15 times.

A 2019 Corvette ZR1 was the pace car at the 2018 Indianapolis 500. It was the 11th Corvette to do so in the past 16 years. The pace cars are production Corvettes that have a special paint job and stickers for the race. They aren't racecars. Corvettes have also been used as pace cars for NASCAR races.

SEVEN-TIME TOUR DE FRANCE WINNER LANCE ARMSTRONG DROVE THE PACE CAR FOR THE 90TH RUNNING OF THE INDIANAPOLIS 500 ON MAY 28, 2006. THIS CORVETTE Z06, BASED ON THE CORVETTE C6.R RACECAR, WAS THE EIGHTH CORVETTE TO SERVE AS AN INDIANAPOLIS 500 PACE CAR.

CHEVROLET

C1
1953–1962

The 1953 Corvette wasn't a powerful car—especially not by today's standards. It was made for cruising and had a 150-horsepower, six-cylinder engine. When the inline six-cylinder engine was replaced with the V-8 engine in 1956, the Corvette's horsepower increased, as did its top speed. Chevrolet also increased the Corvette's production. In 1960, more than 10,000 Corvettes were built.

THIS 1962 CORVETTE HAS FOUR ROUND TAILLIGHTS, WHICH WERE MEANT TO MIRROR ITS FOUR ROUND HEADLIGHTS. THIS WAS THE LAST YEAR OF EXPOSED HEADLIGHTS UNTIL THEIR RETURN IN 2005.

Small changes were made to each model of the C1. For example, in 1954, Chevrolet provided more color choices, including Pennant Blue, Sportsman Red, and black, with the choice of beige, which is a light yellowish-brown color, interior. Before the 1957 model, Corvettes had a three-speed manual transmission, which means the driver has to change gears, or two-speed automatic transmission, which means the car changes gears by itself. The 1957 model offered the choice of a four-speed transmission.

C2
1963–1967

In 1963, the Sting Ray launched the Corvette into its second generation. The 1963 Sting Ray was available both as a coupe and as a convertible. This body style had hidden twin headlights and a split rear window, which only lasted for one model year. The second-generation Corvette's body was designed to be more **aerodynamic** than the models of the first generation. In total, Chevrolet built 21,513 Sting Rays of the 1963 model, 10,594 of which were coupes.

START YOUR ENGINES

IN 1962, CHEVROLET STARTED BUILDING A MODEL OF CORVETTE RACECAR INTENDED TO WIN THE GRAND TOURING, OR GT, CLASS AT THE 24 HOURS OF LE MANS. CHEVROLET CALLED THESE CARS GRAND SPORTS. AFTER FIVE WERE PRODUCED, GM CANCELED THE PROGRAM.

In 1965, the Corvette's engine size increased to 396 cubic inches (6.5 liters). In 1966, it increased to 427 cubic inches (7 liters). The 1967 model is listed as having 430 horsepower, but testing has shown it reaches 500 horsepower or more!

SOME 1963 CORVETTES WERE BUILT WITH **EQUIPMENT** MUCH LIKE THAT OF RACECARS. ONLY 199 CORVETTES OF THIS TYPE WERE MADE.

C3
1968–1982

During the Corvette's third generation, car manufacturing experienced a number of changes. For the first time, car manufacturers began thinking about how their cars affected Earth. The changes Chevrolet made to the Corvette's engine caused the cars to be less powerful. In 1975, the Corvette's engine was only 350 cubic inches (5.7 liters) and only produced 165 horsepower.

The 1968 Sting Ray was heavier than previous models and had a slightly thicker-looking body. This new shape of the car became Corvette's signature, or characteristic mark, from then on. It had a long nose and a small back. Chevrolet made a number of changes to the 1968 Corvette and new parts had to be made for the car. The company only made these parts one year, so there are few parts available for **restoring** these cars. In 1969, the Sting Ray was renamed the Stingray.

THE 1968 CORVETTE HAS A REMOVABLE T-TOP, SHOWN LEFT, WHICH ALLOWED THE COUPE TO HAVE A CONVERTIBLE FEEL.

1974 STINGRAY

C4 AND C5
1984–2004

During the Corvette's fourth and fifth generations, Chevrolet made many changes to the cars. Horsepower increased from 205 in 1984 to 405 in 2004!

At the beginning of the fifth generation, the Corvette was redesigned to include all of the best available technology. The 1997 Corvette was modernized and made more driver friendly but with greater power and speed. The 1997 Corvette had a top speed of 172 miles (276.8 km) per hour. It could go from 0 to 60 miles (0 to 96.6 km) per hour in just 4.7 seconds.

In 1982, the C4 Corvette was introduced as a 1984 model. This means there's no such thing as a 1983 Corvette. The C4 was a total redesign from the C3, and Chevrolet wanted to make sure the car handled better.

EVEN THOUGH THE C4 WAS A TOTAL REDESIGN, CUSTOMERS FOUND THAT IT SQUEAKED AND WAS HARD TO GET IN AND OUT OF.

THE NATIONAL CORVETTE MUSEUM

The National Corvette Museum, located in Bowling Green, Kentucky, opened its doors to the public on September 2, 1994. It houses more than 80 Corvettes from every generation since 1953. The museum displays restored and preserved production models and one-of-a-kind **concept** cars that were never produced and sold. People who have purchased a Corvette can even pick it up from the museum. When visitors come into the museum, they have the chance to get their picture taken sitting in a brand-new Corvette.

C6
2005–2013

The C6 Corvettes are lighter, more powerful, and faster than those from previous generations. They were made to be as powerful as possible while still being allowed to drive on regular roads. A base model C6 Corvette was cheaper than a C5 and had more features. In 2008, Chevrolet introduced the 2009 Corvette ZR1. The ZR1 was the first Corvette that could truly compete with European sports cars in terms of speed and power.

In 2010, the Corvette came in six models: baseline coupe and convertible, Grand Sport coupe and convertible, Z06, and ZR1. This was the second return of the Grand Sport model. It had returned previously in 1996.

Chevrolet celebrated its centennial, or 100th anniversary, in 2012. To mark the occasion, Chevrolet presented the Centennial **Edition** package, which included a special paint job, wheels, badges, and interior.

THE 2012 ZR1 HAS A 378 CUBIC INCH (6.2 LITER) ENGINE AND 638 HORSEPOWER! IT HAS A TOP SPEED OF 205 MILES (329.9 KM) PER HOUR. AT THE TIME, IT WAS THE FASTEST, MOST POWERFUL CAR EVER MADE BY GENERAL MOTORS.

THE C6.R GT2

In 2010, Chevrolet introduced the newest Corvette racecar—the C6.R GT2. Corvette Racing based the GT2 on the ZR1 sports car and the two cars have many similarities, such as their body designs. However, the C6.R has to follow certain rules and must have a less powerful engine than the ZR1. The C6.R competes against European racecars, such as Ferraris, Porsches, and Aston Martins, in GT races in the ALMS.

C7
2014–PRESENT

On January 13, 2013, at an invitation-only reveal in Detroit, Michigan, the seventh-generation Corvette was introduced with the Stingray name, which hadn't appeared on a Corvette since the third generation. The C7 features a new crossed-flags logo but kept its front-engine, rear-wheel-drive platform. It has a new V-8 engine that produces 455 horsepower and can go from 0 to 60 miles (0 to 96.6 km) per hour in 3.8 seconds. The 2014 Z06's V-8 engine produced 650 horsepower.

The C7 Corvette designs make it look longer and sleeker than other sports cars, such as the Porsche 911. This also makes the C7 Corvettes more aerodynamic. A new chassis, or frame, allows the C7 Corvette to handle better and take tighter corners. It is the most fuel-**efficient** Corvette ever produced.

SOME CORVETTE ENTHUSIASTS HAVE CRITICIZED, OR FOUND FAULT WITH, SOME PARTS OF THE C7 CORVETTE'S DESIGN. THE C7'S TAILLIGHTS, WHICH ARE SIMILAR TO THE FIFTH-GENERATION CHEVROLET CAMARO'S TAILLIGHTS, STRAY FROM THE CORVETTE'S FAMOUS ROUND TAILLIGHTS.

THE CORVETTE LOGO

Over the years, the Corvette's crossed-flags logo has changed eight times. The original logo featured a checkered flag on the right and an American flag on the left, which was against federal law because the flag couldn't be used for advertising. This flag was changed out for a red flag with the Chevrolet logo and a fleur-de-lis to honor Louis Chevrolet's French background. The fleur-de-lis is a symbol, or something that stands for something else, of France. You can only see the original Corvette logo on display at the National Corvette Museum.

THE FUTURE OF THE CORVETTE

The Corvette is a symbol of American design, engineering, and innovation. Throughout the years, Corvettes have remained an American classic.

As of 2018, Chevrolet is working on the eighth generation of Corvettes, which will be known as the C8. The C8 will be mid-engined, which means its engine will sit between the seats and the rear wheels. This design is completely new for the brand.

Even though General Motors has been very secretive about what this new generation will look like and what kind of power it will have, this Corvette will stay true to its roots as an affordable sports car with high performance. It's expected to be slightly heavier than the C7s and have a similar engine, but it's also expected to produce around 500 horsepower. This completely new design will launch the Corvette into the future of sports cars.

OVER THE YEARS, CHEVROLET HAS PRODUCED AND DISPLAYED A NUMBER OF CONCEPT CORVETTES. ON FEBRUARY 15, 2009, THIS CORVETTE STINGRAY CONCEPT CAR WAS DISPLAYED AT THE CHICAGO AUTO SHOW IN CHICAGO, ILLINOIS.

TIMELINE

January 17, 1953 › A Corvette show car is revealed at the GM Motorama at the Waldorf Astoria Hotel in New York City.

June 30, 1953 › The first Corvette is produced in Flint, Michigan. Only 300 units are made.

1963 › The C2 Corvette is released as the Sting Ray. This is the first and only year of the split rear window.

1968 › The C3 Corvette is released.

1969 › The Stingray name returns as one word.

1984 › The C4 Corvette is released. No Stingrays are produced during this generation.

1994 › The National Corvette Museum opens to the public.

1997 › The C5 Corvette is released. It is only offered as a coupe during this model year.

2001 › The Z06 model is introduced.

2005 › The C6 Corvette is released.

2009 › The ZR1 model is introduced.

2010 › The Grand Sport model returns for the second time.

2012 › Chevrolet celebrates its 100th anniversary.

2014 › The C7 Corvette is released.

GLOSSARY

aerodynamic: The qualities of an object that affect how easily it's able to move through the air.

concept: Organized around a main idea or theme; created to show a general idea.

cylinder: A tube-shaped part of an engine where power is created.

design: The way something has been made. Also, to create the plan for something.

edition: One of the forms in which something is presented.

efficient: Capable of producing wanted results without wasting materials, time, or energy.

equipment: Supplies or tools needed for a certain purpose.

passenger: Someone riding on or in a vehicle.

professional: Having to do with a job someone does for a living.

restore: To return something to an earlier or original condition by repairing it, cleaning it, etc.

technology: The way people do something and the tools they use.

transmission: The part of a car or another vehicle that uses the engine's power to turn the wheels.

INDEX

WEBSITES

Due to the changing nature of Internet links, PowerKids Press has developed an online list of websites related to the subject of this book. This site is updated regularly. Please use this link to access the list: www.powerkidslinks.com/hood/corvettes